Mechanic Mike's M[...] Diggers

A+
Smart Apple Media

Published by Smart Apple Media, an imprint of Black Rabbit Books
P.O. Box 3263, Mankato, Minnesota 56002
www.blackrabbitbooks.com

Produced by David West 🏃 Children's Books
6 Princeton Court, 55 Felsham Road, London SW15 1AZ

Designed and illustrated by David West

Copyright © 2014 David West Children's Books

Library of Congress Cataloging-in-Publication Data

West, David, 1956-
 Diggers / David West.
    pages cm – (Mechanic Mike's machines)
 Includes index.
 Audience: K to grade 3.
 ISBN 978-1-62588-062-8 (library binding)
 ISBN 978-1-62588-101-4 (paperback)
1. Earthmoving machinery–Juvenile literature. I. Title.
 TA725.W28 2013
 621.8'65–dc23
                              2013032021

                       Printed in China
            CPSIA compliance information: DWCB14CP
                          010114

                    9 8 7 6 5 4 3 2 1

Mechanic Mike says:
This little guy will tell
you something more
about the machine.

 Find out what type
of engine drives
the machine.

 Discover
something you
didn't know.

 Size dimensions
are supplied here.

 Find out how
heavy it is.

 Get your
amazing
fact here!

Contents

Bulldozer

These powerful, large earth movers are usually first on a new work site. They push away debris and piles of earth and rocks.

Giant **diesel engines** power the drive wheel at the back of the machine.

Did you know bulldozers have a giant ripper at the back? They use this to tear up tree roots, boulders, concrete, and asphalt.

These massive machines are over 30 feet (9.1 m) long.

Bulldozers can weigh up to 100 tons (90 metric tons). That's the same as 15 African elephants.

Bulldozers with air-conditioned sealed cabs are used to help fight wildfires. They can push vegetation out of the way to stop the fire from spreading.

Mechanic Mike says:
Crawler tracks, also called caterpillar tracks, allow the bulldozer to move over rough, uneven ground.

5

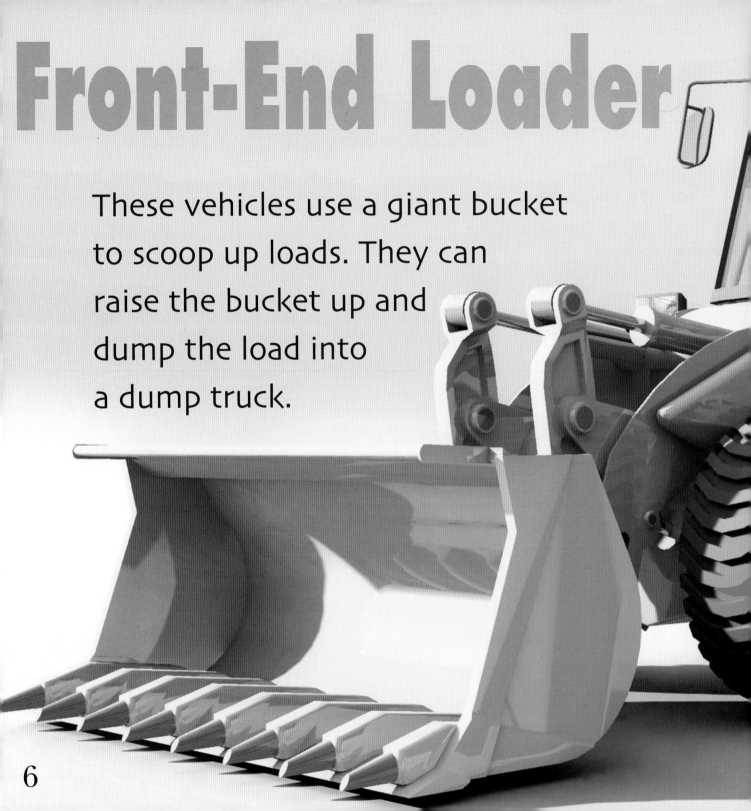

Front-End Loader

These vehicles use a giant bucket to scoop up loads. They can raise the bucket up and dump the load into a dump truck.

These vehicles use powerful diesel engines to drive the wheels.

Did you know the largest rubber-tired, front-end wheel loader in the world is the Le Tourneau's L-2350? Its bucket can carry more than 400 tons (363 metric tons).

This medium-sized vehicle is 24.6 feet (7.5 m) long.

It weighs 19 tons (17.2 metric tons). That's about three African elephants.

Front-end loaders are also called bucket loader, pay loader and scoop shovel.

Mechanic Mike says:
Unlike most bulldozers, most front-end loaders are wheeled and not tracked.

7

Backhoe

These tractor-like diggers can do many different jobs. They have a bucket on the front and a backhoe digger at the back. Stabilizer arms at the rear keep it level when it digs.

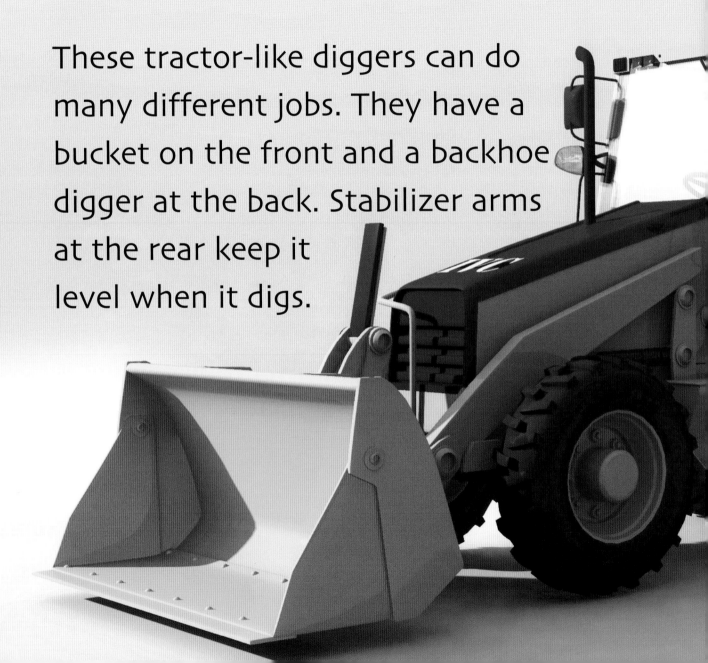

The bucket on the back can be replaced with other tools, such as a drill, or **grapple**.

Did you know the machine usually has a seat that can swivel backward to use the backhoe controls?

This machine weighs 8.5 tons (7.7 metric tons). That's slightly more than a large African elephant.

Backhoe loaders are typically about 20 feet (6 m) long.

It has a diesel engine that powers the wheels and the **hydraulic rams**.

Mechanic Mike says:
Backhoe is the shortened name for backhoe loader. They are also called JCBs after the company that invented them.

The large diesel engine powers the drive wheels for the tracks as well as for the hydraulics.

Did you know the arm and bucket are powered by hydraulic cylinders? Liquid is forced into a cylinder which pushes a ramrod that moves the hinged arm.

Medium-sized excavators like this one are around 50 feet (15.2 m) long with the arm extended.

It weighs 34.5 tons (31.3 metric tons). That's the same as about five African elephants.

Excavators are also called 360-degree excavators. This is because the cab and arm unit, called the "house," can rotate all the way around.

Mechanic Mike says:
Excavators can also be used for demolition work. Their long arms are ideal for pulling down the walls of houses and offices.

Excavator

Excavators are used on construction sites. Their powerful arms with claw-like buckets are used to dig out trenches and foundations.

Scraper

These strange-looking machines are usually seen on highway construction sites. They scrape over the earth and carry away the soil.

Mechanic Mike says:
The soil it has collected might be unloaded gradually to fill hollows or released in a huge pile to make embankments.

To slice into the earth, a giant scraper is lowered 12 inches (30 cm) into the ground. It acts like a giant butter knife.

 They can weigh up to 53 tons (48 metric tons). That's over six African elephants.

 Scrapers are long vehicles measuring up to 50 feet (15.2 m) long.

 These powerful machines have two diesel engines. One at the front powers the cab. The second is at the back and powers the rear wheels.

 Did you know that scrapers often get stuck and need a bulldozer to push them out?

Compactor

Compactors are used to compress earth, gravel, or asphalt during the construction of a road or highway.

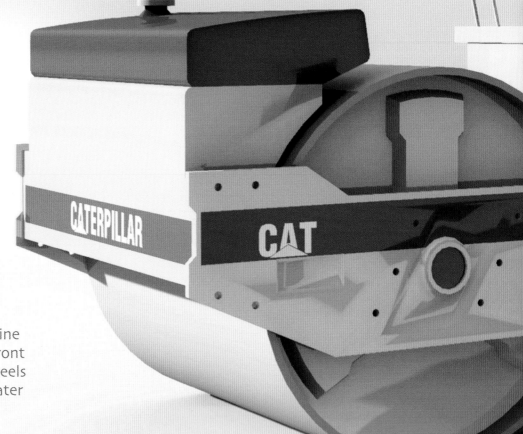

Mechanic Mike says:
Weight is added to the machine by filling large tanks at the front and back with water. The wheels themselves may also have water added for extra weight.

This machine uses a diesel engine.

Did you know water may be sprinkled on the drums from on-board tanks to prevent hot asphalt from sticking to the drum?

Some units may weigh 21 tons (19 metric tons). That's three elephants!

Drums range from 24 to 84 inches (0.6 to 2 meters) in width.

Rollers may also vibrate to help settle the material they are compacting.

Mini Excavator

Some diggers are built in smaller sizes. They can work in places that larger machines cannot fit. They are mainly used to dig trenches for pipes, and cables along roadsides.

Mechanic Mike says:
These smaller machines have a small dozer blade at the front to move soil and rubble.

16

Smaller excavators are powered by diesel engines.

Did you know two small levers on each side are used to control the excavating arm?

They weigh around 9.4 tons (8.5 metric tons).

This machine measures under 10 feet (3 m) in length.

To protect their ears, drivers must wear ear plugs when they work on these machines.

Skid Steer

This machine can work in small spaces. By reversing its wheels on one side and driving forward on the other, it can spin around on its axis.

Mechanic Mike says:
Like many machines in this book, the skid steer can change the tool on its arm to perform other tasks.

18

The skid steer is powered by a small diesel engine.

Did you know that skid steers don't have steering wheels? They have hand levers to steer with.

It weighs 0.8 tons (0.76 metric tons).

The skid steer measures around 10 feet (3 m) long.

Skid steers can be used to dig with a bucket or lift things with a forklift attachment. It even has a brush for sweeping up.

19

Mining Shovel

These massive diggers are used to cut away seams of coal or oil shale from the walls of open-pit mines. The massive bucket has replaceable, self-sharpening teeth which bite into the rock.

Did you know that this mining shovel can fill the back of a giant **dump truck** in under two minutes?

 This machine is 44 feet (13.4 m) long.

 Mining shovels like this one can weigh up to 472 tons (480 metric tons). That's about 65 large African elephants.

 Mining shovels have two large diesel engines. If one breaks down it can still run on one while the other is being repaired.

 It can run at full speed for three hours.

LIEBHERR 962

Mechanic Mike says: These machines use computers that measure and control the engine and the shovel. When a tooth wears out it is replaced.

21

Bucket-Wheel

Bucket-wheel excavators (BWEs) are used as continuous digging machines in large-scale open pit mining operations. A large wheel of buckets scoops up material as the wheel turns.

 These machines can move 8.51 million cubic feet (240,000 cubic meters) of earth per day.

 Did you know BWEs are the largest moving land machines ever built?

 A combination of diesel and electric engines are used to power this mighty machine.

 They weigh in at 15,653 tons (14,200 metric tons). That's a lot of elephants!

BWEs can be 314.9 feet (96 m) tall and are 738.2 feet (225 m) long.

Excavator

Mechanic Mike says:
Each bucket-wheel is over 70 feet (21.3 m) across, which can hold the equivalent of 80 bathtubs of material.

Glossary

diesel engines
Engines using diesel fuel.

dump truck
A truck used for transporting rock and earth.

grapple
A hook or claw used to catch or hold something.

hydraulic ram
A device on a machine that acts like a mechanical muscle. Fluid is pumped in one end, which pushes out a piston. When fluid is pumped in at the other end it pushes the piston back. The moving piston moves a mechanical arm backward and forward.

Index

24